IMAGES
of America

PRESCOTT VALLEY

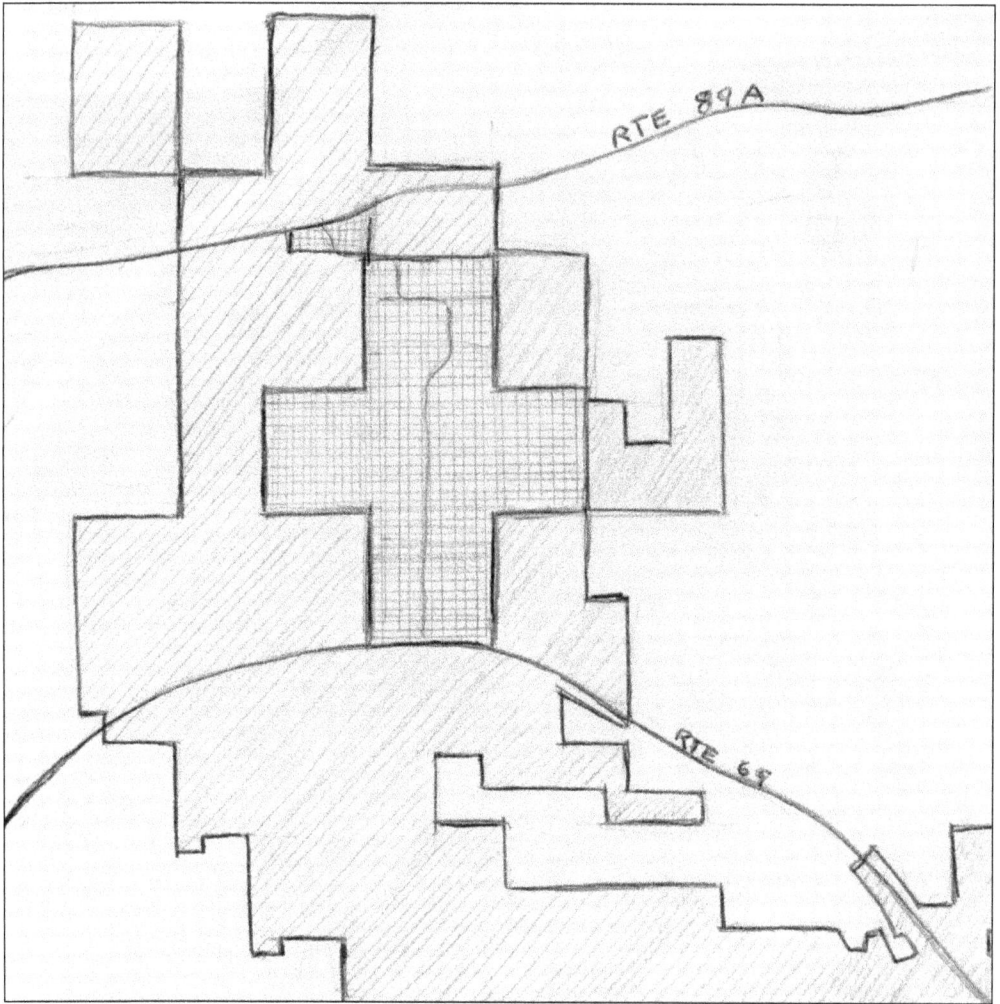

Prescott Valley has seen phenomenal growth in its 42 years. Begun in 1966, it has grown to an established community of 38,000 people. It is situated in a wide-open valley bordered by the Bradshaw Mountains to the south, the Black Hills to the east, and Glassford Hill to the west. The first territorial capital of Prescott is 8 miles away, and the state capital of Phoenix is 80 miles to the south. Prescott Valley has a history of Paleolithic, prehistoric, and historic events. It was mining and ranching that brought settlers to the area, and today it is the lifestyle that attracts both young and old. At 5,100 feet, the climate is mild, with four seasons and easy access to the desert in the south and snow-capped peaks to the north. The map above depicts the growth of the town from its beginnings of five sections of land to the extensive addition of surrounding areas. (Author rendering.)

ON THE COVER: Early residents came to Prescott Valley to taste the spirit of the West on land that was once home to cowboys and their herds of cattle. A corral was provided for those with horses, and the strip mall took on the appearance of an old Western town. Hitching rails and watering troughs were placed in front of shops for those customers who arrived on horseback. (Sandra Sasser.)

IMAGES
of America

PRESCOTT VALLEY

Jean Cross

ARCADIA
PUBLISHING

Published by Arcadia Publishing
Charleston SC, Chicago IL, Portsmouth NH, San Francisco CA

Library of Congress Catalog Card Number: 2008938758

For all general information contact Arcadia Publishing at:
Telephone 843-853-2070
Fax 843-853-0044
E-mail sales@arcadiapublishing.com
For customer service and orders:
Toll-Free 1-888-313-2665

Visit us on the Internet at www.arcadiapublishing.com

This book is dedicated to all those people
who came to Lonesome Valley to find the life they were seeking.
This includes the prehistoric people, the miners, the ranchers and
farmers, and today's population.

CONTENTS

ACKNOWLEDGMENTS

Many people have helped to make this book possible. I am especially grateful to Don Cunningham, who not only trusted me with his laptop but taught me how to use it. He was always there to rescue me as I fumbled my way through computer basics. Many friends and acquaintances offered photographs in my search for the pictures seen in the book. Jerry Munderloh made his research notes, books, and photographs available. Darcy Morger Grovenstein drove me around the area photographing today's buildings. Bill Fain provided the photographs for the chapter on ranching. Stew Schrauger opened his professional files for my use. Nigel Reynolds offered his photographs of historic trails, as did Tracy and Judy DeVault. Earl ("Beaver") Neville and the Jeffries family added their collections of early Prescott Valley photographs. The town of Prescott Valley provided photographs and much encouragement. Sharlot Hall Museum also provided photographs. And my thanks are also extended to Jared Jackson of Arcadia Publishing, whose patience and encouragement were always there to urge me on and provide help when needed. A heartfelt thank-you goes to all who helped to make this publication possible. Dates, names, locations, and other facts are deemed to be accurate but not guaranteed. We welcome documented corrections and other input for future additions.

INTRODUCTION

What was once a peaceful, quiet valley has actually been witness to two rather violent eruptions in its long history. The first was when the land was covered with volcanic ash and lava as the hill to the west erupted, forming Glassford Hill. Another eruption occurred more recently as the town of Prescott Valley arose from a placid ranch land to a town of more than 35,000 people in the short span of only 40 years.

From its first eruption, which occurred some 10 million years ago, to the present time, the area has had a varied occupation. Mammoths once roamed through the lush grasses, as did prehistoric horses, camels, and sloths. With the advent of man in the region, people known today as the Prescott Culture found the valley to their liking. Water, food, and material for shelter were readily available to them. They enjoyed a rather peaceful existence until gold was discovered in the mountains in 1863.

With the influx of the miners, another less violent eruption took place as these people sought to make their fortunes in the lands once belonging to the Native Americans. The military arrived, as did entrepreneurs who also came to seek their fortunes in supplying the needs of the growing population.

The Walker party entered the area about 1863 and set up their claims along Lynx Creek and the Hassayampa River. The Bradshaw Mountains became a virtual honeycomb of diggings as the miners searched for precious metals.

This was the time of the Civil War, and the North was depleting its treasury in the pursuit of victory over the South. It was determined that the capital of the Arizona territory should be located near the newly discovered goldfields. A governmental party was formed and arrived in the area in 1864. The capital, named Prescott, was established along Granite Creek, and Fort Whipple was moved from Del Rio to a location near the capital.

It was not long before ranchers, merchants, and others sought to make their living in supplying the needs of the new community. Ready markets were found among the miners, the military, and the settlers. Freighters carried supplies from the Colorado River across long and desolate trails. Danger from marauding bands, lack of water, and great inconveniences were ever present, but some found this occupation even more lucrative than searching for precious metals.

With the arrival of the automobile in the early 20th century, more convenient means of transportation became necessary. Trails became graded and paved roads. Population in the arid Southwest began to increase following World War II, and Arizona became a destination for residents and tourists alike.

Norman Fain, an Arizona state senator in the 1940s, saw the need for building a more direct route between Phoenix and Flagstaff. By the mid-1950s, such a highway had reached as far as present-day Cordes Junction. It seemed advisable at that point to connect Prescott to the new highway, and thus Route 69 was constructed. This new road passed through the communities of Mayer, Humboldt, and Dewey, crossing the Fain Ranch on its way to Prescott.

It was not long before this open valley caught the eye of Ned Warren. Warren had become known for his many questionable development schemes across the country. However, he began negotiations with Fain in the mid-1960s that began the town of Prescott Valley. Warren ultimately moved on to a similar deal near Kingman, Arizona, and left Prescott Valley in the hands of Robert Loos and Leonard Hoffman. These two began peddling property throughout the country, offering a steak dinner and a presentation extolling the wonders of the West.

Attendees must have been convinced of the worthiness of these claims, as they purchased property sight unseen. As residents began to arrive, the new company known as Prescott Valley, Inc., saw fit to offer fringe benefits to placate them. A motel and restaurant were built to accommodate the visitors when they came to view their property. A gas station, an activity building, and a strip mall were eventually constructed. Property owners were offered leases in these buildings to open businesses to provide the necessities of life in the new community. A park and swimming pool were among the fringe benefits, and a monthly newsletter was published to acquaint the people on the progress of their new home. This publication was appropriately named *Fringe Benefit*.

A post office was opened in 1969 as well as a grocery store and a fast food shop called the Valley Hut. Great Western Bank appeared in 1971, and Safeway built its plaza in 1978. That year also saw the incorporation of the town. Industries began to locate in Prescott Valley. Better Built Aluminum and Print Pack were among the first to take advantage of the new town location. An elementary school was opened in 1972 and a high school in 1976. The first church service was held in the A Frame building but was soon moved to the Open Door Baptist Church, the first church built in the valley. The dirt roads were soon beginning to be paved and a security system and fire department installed.

Since these beginnings, Prescott Valley has experienced phenomenal growth. It has attracted numerous industries; public elementary, middle, and high schools as well as charter schools; over 30 churches; and two higher education institutions. Public parks and its proximity to the Prescott National Forest offer unlimited opportunities for recreation. The newly opened entertainment district and sports arena offer additional options for leisure-time activities.

In an effort to preserve its history, an Old Town board was organized in 2006 to establish an Old Town district. The buildings constructed by Prescott Valley, Inc., are targeted to become a destination for tourists and residents alike. An area behind the strip mall is designated to be a park to be enjoyed by visitors and to be the scene of community programs. In its location along Highway 69, it enjoys excellent exposure to travelers along the road seeking to taste the flavor of the West, which once attracted the original residents to this part of Arizona.

One

PREHISTORY OF
PRESCOTT VALLEY

Prescott Valley has a long and varied history going back millions of years. Seeing the sprawling city of today, it is difficult to imagine a valley bombarded by the eruption of a volcano at the site of Glassford Hill. It did erupt some 10 million years ago, spewing its lava far and wide. As recently as 1,000 years ago, Sunset Crater in the Flagstaff area erupted. Evidence of its ashes is found in prehistoric ruins built shortly after its eruption.

About 10,000 years ago, the area was covered with lush vegetation, and mammoths and other prehistoric mammals found the valley to their liking. In 1984, a hiker walking the Aqua Fria Wash noticed bones protruding from the banks and notified authorities. These remains proved to be mammoth bones and a portion of a tusk. Mastodon remains have been found to the southwest in the Prescott National Forest.

Other inhabitants claimed the valley as their home about 1,500 years ago. Those known as the Prescott Culture once built dwellings here. They settled in extended family groups living in pit houses. A few pueblos were built, which are believed to have been gathering places for neighboring groups. The Fitzmaurice Ruin in Fain Park is an example of this type of dwelling. It consists of a 27-room pueblo with 24 outlier rooms.

Prescott Valley is the location of many prehistoric sites, and artifacts may be found throughout the valley. In wandering along the numerous trails and roads in the vicinity, one can imagine the types of habitations that once existed here. Large mammals such as the mammoth waded through the tall grasses. Hunters and gatherers of later times took advantage of the wildlife and available berries and nuts as they strove to eke out a living in the valley.

Like a sleeping giant, Glassford Hill looms over Prescott Valley to the west of town. Once an active volcano, it has been dormant for some 10 million years. Most of the mountain is state trust land today. It is leased to ranchers, but development is beginning to encroach upon its slopes. (Author collection.)

Though Glassford Hill erupted long ago, a recent sunset photographed by the author gave somewhat the impression of an eruption. (Author collection.)

In 1984, a hiker walking along the Agua Fria Wash noticed large bones and a partial tusk protruding from its banks. He notified authorities, and upon examination, it was confirmed that these were the remains of a mammoth. Further excavation of the area revealed prehistoric horse and camel remains. (Darcy Morger Grovenstein.)

The Agua Fria Wash crosses Prescott Valley to the north. A recent visit to the area brought forth visions of mammoths and other prehistoric animals roaming the wide expanse of Lonesome Valley. The valley is still the scene of grazing animals in the form of cattle, pronghorn, and deer. (Darcy Morger Grovenstein.)

The valley was once the scene of more recent prehistoric habitation. Evidence of this can be found throughout the valley. Chief among these remains is the Fitzmaurice Ruins in Fain Park. On a hill across the lake, prehistoric people built a 27-room pueblo with 24 outlier rooms. It is thought to have been a gathering place for neighboring people, since such structures were rare in the area. This picture shows Sharlot Hall (at right in foreground) visiting the ruins. (Sharlot Hall Museum.)

Other evidence of early habitation can be found in the petroglyphs that adorn boulders. Though no one has been able to interpret the meaning of these inscriptions, they testify to the ability of the artists and their ingenuity in leaving lasting evidence of their existence. (Author collection.)

12

Clay pots, such as this bowl, are typical of the work of the people of the Prescott Culture. These people were hunters and gatherers who roamed the area in search for food. Their ceramics were mainly utilitarian in nature, and potsherds are found throughout the valley. (Author collection.)

Fetishes are also found in the habitation sites of the Prescott Culture. These are thought to be ceremonial objects and sometimes take the form of more human representation. Some could even have been made as toys for children. (Author collection.)

Excavations of prehistoric sites are carried on by professional and avocational archaeologists. Pictured here are crew members excavating a midden or trash mound in a site near Willow Lake. Such excavations are carefully recorded, and photographs are taken of various aspects of the work. (Author collection.)

With the discovery of gold in north-central Arizona in the mid-19th century and the subsequent arrival of miners and settlers, the native population found their lands being inhabited by strangers. Struggles to retain possession of these lands proved impossible, and they finally resigned themselves to be placed on reservations. One of the leaders of the Yavapai tribe proved herself to be a calming influence for her people. Viola Jimula succeeded her husband, Sam Jimula, to become chieftess of her people and helped them to adjust to this new way of life. (Sharlot Hall Museum.)

The Yavapai are known for their skill in weaving baskets. Here Viola is seen engaging in this traditional art. Baskets were essential equipment for early hunters and gatherers as they roamed the area for the necessities of life. (Sharlot Hall Museum.)

Dwellings such as this early hut have since been replaced by more substantial housing on today's Yavapai Reservation, which is adjacent to the Veterans' Hospital. At one time, it was part of the Fort Whipple property until designated as the reservation. (Sharlot Hall Museum.)

This statue at the entrance of the Prescott Resort commemorates the strength and perseverance of the early Yavapai. The Yavapai people now operate a casino adjacent to the resort. Both the resort and the casino are located on the Yavapai Reservation. (Author collection.)

Two

THE LURE OF GOLD

The comparative peace of these early inhabitants was to become disrupted with the arrival of the Walker party. Joseph Walker had traversed the West since early in the 19th century. Daniel Connor recorded the journey of Walker and his party into Arizona in their search for gold.

Ragged and bedraggled, short of supplies, and enduring great thirst, the newcomers first settled along the Hassayampa River in the spring of 1863. Later, while prospecting neighboring streams, the party settled on Lynx Creek, where the placer diggings proved more abundant.

In establishing a capital for the Arizona territory, the North wanted to take advantage of the newly discovered gold deposits to replenish the heavy losses sustained during the Civil War. The capital, therefore, was established in nearby Prescott in 1864.

The miners, having usurped the lands of the natives who had lived there for centuries, needed the protection of the military. An army fort had been established at Del Rio in Chino Valley. Later a location for the capital and the fort was selected along Granite Creek.

The quest for gold continued on through the remainder of the 19th century. So it was that people from the east sought their fortunes in the goldfields of Arizona. Among them was the Hall family, arriving in 1882. James Hall, father of Sharlot Hall, engaged not only in mining but also in ranching and farming. Lonesome Valley also became the home of an engaging young Englishman named Thomas Gibson Barlow Massicks. He built an impressive Victorian home along Lynx Creek known to present-day residents as "the Castle." Barlow Massicks carried on an impressive array of mining activities along Lynx Creek until his untimely death in 1899.

Gold is still the lure of some of today's residents, and one can often see hunched figures panning for bits of "color" along area streams.

Early miners entering the Arizona territory in search for gold brought everything with them on the backs of mules or packhorses. Here one of them stops to rest his animals on his trek to stake a claim. (Sharlot Hall Museum.)

Gold panners tried their luck along the streams. It appears that these two fortune seekers are actually trying to see if there is gold in this stream. (Sharlot Hall Museum.)

Sharlot Hall and her family are shown here trying their luck with a gold pan along Lynx Creek. Sharlot's father, James, was a miner as well as a rancher and farmer. (Sharlot Hall Museum.)

With the discovery of gold in the region in 1863, word spread quickly, and miners sought their fortunes in the mountains and along the streams. Openings such as this began to appear in the hillsides as miners looked for elusive veins of the precious metal. (Author collection.)

Ore cars were piled high with excavation material and transported the ore-bearing rock from the tunnels to be taken to the mill for processing. (Author collection.)

Machinery was hauled across the deserts and put into place to ease the task of extracting the refuse from the mines. This wench and cable are part of a mining exhibit in Fain Park. (Author collection.)

Hydraulic mining was one means of extracting the ore. Diversion dams and ditches were built to carry water downstream to be attached to hoses, which washed down the banks of the stream. This dam is located on Lynx Creek. (Jerry Munderloh.)

Ditches were dug in which the diverted water flowed. This ditch can still be seen along Lynx Creek, although its flow is now used for other purposes. (Darcy Morger Grovenstein.)

21

A ditch funneled water along the south side of Lynx Creek to flow into 30-inch pipes and then to smaller pipes to build up pressure for hydraulic mining. (Jerry Munderloh.)

The pipe and ditch can be seen here as they descended toward the Fain Lake dam. Sections of the pipe are still evident, as is the ditch, which once carried water downstream to be used in a hydraulic mining operation. (Jerry Munderloh.)

A smaller pipe funneled water across the dam to the site of the hydraulic mining operation. The Barlow Massicks house can be seen here above Lynx Creek. (Jerry Munderloh.)

Fain Lake Dam, built for early mining on Lynx Creek, still stands below the Castle. Sections of the 30-inch pipe and the ditch can be seen in the background. (Author collection.)

The lake created by the dam once held a dredge. Debris from the lake bottom was dredged up to be crushed by mills to extract the gold. (Sharlot Hall Museum.)

This valve is believed to have been located in the dam and used to release water when necessary. It is on display in Fain Park. (Author collection.)

Farther up Lynx Creek, an 8,000-foot tunnel was dug through the mountain for ore cars to transport ore to a mill in Poland. (Sharlot Hall Museum.)

This stamp mill was once in use on Lynx Creek about a quarter of a mile upstream from Fain Park. A fire destroyed its supporting timbers, but it has been restored and is now on exhibit in the park. (Sharlot Hall Museum.)

This wheel once lifted the stamps of the mill and was restored and placed in Fain Park. The mill was originally manufactured in San Francisco and was transported to Lonesome Valley. (Author collection.)

A portion of Fain Park has been set aside for a mining exhibit to acquaint the public with the history of the early mining operations that took place along the creek. Interpretive signs explain the use of each piece of equipment. The exhibit is the work of Jerry Munderloh and Jean Cross. (Author collection.)

The "Castle," the home of Barlow Massicks, still stands above Lynx Creek. It was built about 1890. This young man built the house as he carried on mining operations in the area. The house is part of the 100 acres of park property donated by the Fain family to the Town of Prescott Valley. (Author collection.)

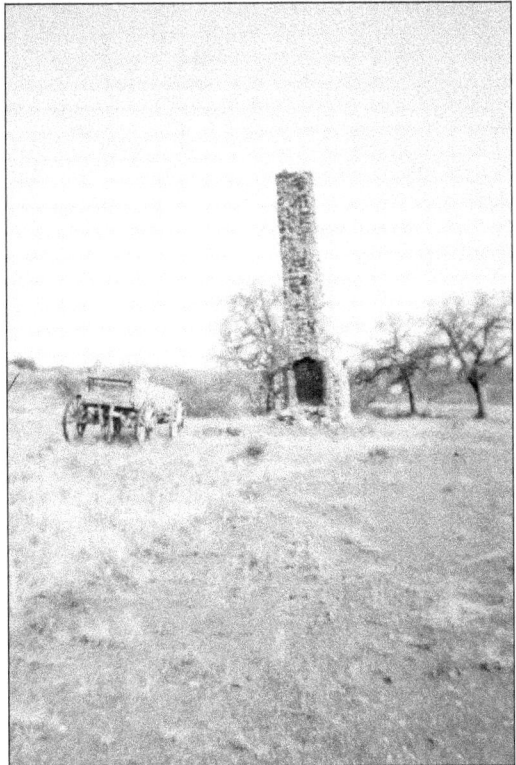

This chimney still stands in the yard near the Castle and is believed to have been in the general store in the town of Massicks. The store was also the location of a stage stop and post office. At one time, Barlow Massicks was the postmaster. (Author collection.)

The area around the park also contains several short trails and nature areas. Members of the Key Club of Bradshaw Mountain High School and their sponsors are seen here after a day of clean-up and maintenance of the exhibit and trails. From left to right are (first row) Melissa Montgomery, Emory Grovenstein, and Darcy Grovenstein; (second row) Andrew Bickert, Zeke Grovenstein, Ashley Gohr, Sean Thatcher, Candace Gorsky, Glen Grovenstein, Jack Caward, and Jean Cross. (Jerry Munderloh.)

Three

VALLEY RANCHES

Mammoths once grazed in Lonesome Valley, and later, pronghorn, deer, and small rodents feasted on the lush grasses. Some of the first settlers were able to supplement their incomes by cutting these grasses and selling bales of them to the military at Fort Whipple. Finally the valley was the scene of herds of cattle as ranchers ran their livestock there.

As the population around the territorial capital increased, supplies were more in demand. Ranches and farms became more abundant to supply the needs of settlers, miners, merchants, and the military. Beef, hides, and tallow were much sought after by the newcomers, as was fresh produce. As with mining and freighting, these occupations were fraught with dangers from marauding bands.

In order to supply the needs of the growing territory, some ranchers engaged in other pursuits as well. Thomas Sanders ran cattle in the Yaeger Canyon area and also freighted supplies across the mountain to Jerome. James Hall engaged in farming and fruit growing on his spread, appropriately called Orchard Ranch. Sharlot Hall once delivered produce from her family's ranch to townspeople and to miners. The Fains still engage in ranching in the valley.

Once railroads crossed the country, goods could be shipped more easily in and out of the territory. Ranchers acquired more land, increased their herds, and shipped their beef throughout the country. Life on the range became somewhat easier. At roundup each year, the cowboys engaged in riding and roping competitions, and thus the rodeo became a yearly event.

There were good times and hard times brought on by droughts and depressions. Hearty ones survived, and some families are still in the cattle business today. Some have seen opportunities in selling part of their holdings to developers, but cattle are still an important industry in Arizona.

One of the first ranchers in the new territory was King Woolsey. His ranch was located off the Old Black Canyon Highway between today's Dewey and Humboldt. The Woolsey ranch house was constructed from remains of a prehistoric ruin. Some of the walls of the ruin can be seen here. Woolsey was known for his forays with the native people when they engaged in stealing cattle. (Author collection.)

The Fain family arrived in 1874 and settled in the Verde Valley. When William and Cary Fain reached Arizona, they were short on supplies and weary from their long journey. William began to cut grass and sell it to the military in order to earn money. Later he acquired land near Cornville and established a ranch. One of their first encampments is shown here. (Fain family.)

Lonesome Valley became the location of several ranches. Among them were the Langs, the Sanders, and the Halls. Dan Fain, son of William and Cary, also ran cattle here. Since no fences existed at that time, roundups were carried on to gather and sort the cattle for branding and shipping. (Fain family.)

Long hours were spent in riding the range and the forests to collect the strays and lead them to the roundup. This scene became a familiar site at that time. (Fain family.)

After locating stray cattle, cowboys are seen here as they led them to the place of roundup, where they were paired with their calves. (Fain family.)

Cutting cattle was the process of sorting out the various herds and pairing calves with their mothers. The calves were then roped and branded. (Fain family.)

The scene of a branding was a rather raucous event, as cowboys shouted out and calves bellowed. But the branded calves were soon set free to rejoin their mothers. (Fain family.)

Pictured here is a roundup on the ML Ranch. Cowboys enjoy some respite after a long day in the saddle looking for strays and leading them home. (Fain family.)

Dan Fain's first brand was acquired at the age of five when he roped his first calf. When asked what brand he wanted, he yelled "Hey" and thus acquired the HA brand. Later Dan and partner Kooge Wilkins owned the ML Ranch and renamed it the Rafter Eleven. That brand is pictured here. (Fain family.)

Cattle are seen here being herded into corrals awaiting selection for shipping. A train is seen in the background ready to take them to market. (Fain family.)

The selected cattle are led into chutes to be loaded onto railroad cars. In earlier days, cattle drives were carried on to transport cattle to market. (Fain family.)

After the roundup, the cutting of cattle, the branding, and the shipping of selected cows, ranchers get together at a "summit meeting" to discuss the work and make future plans. (Fain family.)

Cowboys also gather and enjoy a rest from their labors. They are seen here engaging in some bantering, yarns, and tales of their adventures. (Fain family.)

Cattle and their calves not selected for shipping are set free to roam once again in their search for food on the range. (Fain family.)

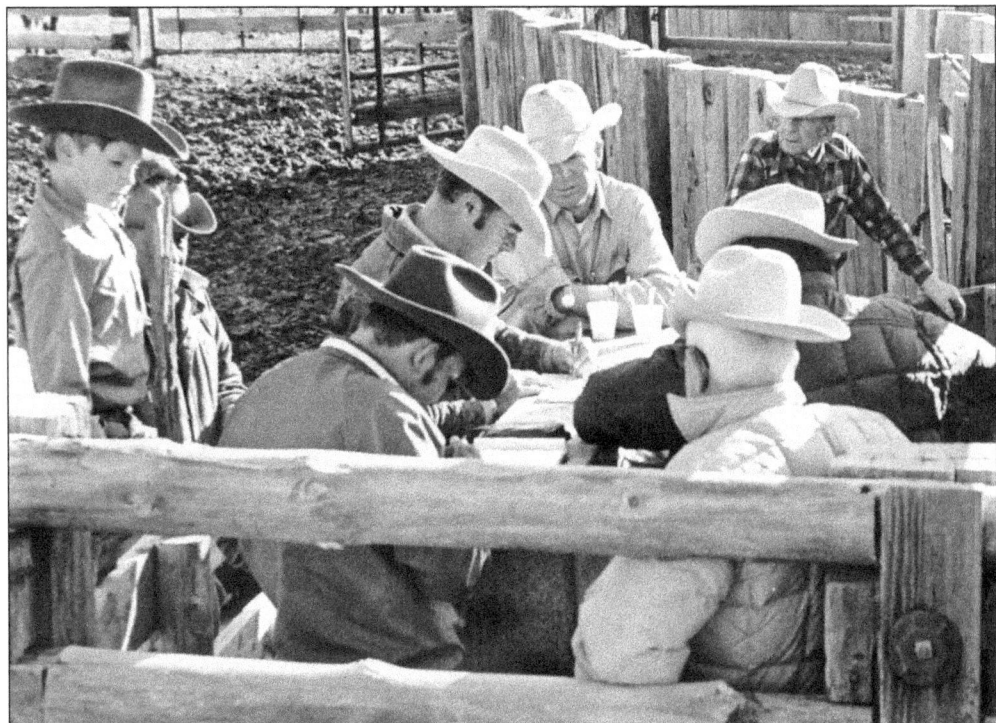

Ranchers also meet to "tally up the take" and discuss ranch business to be faced in the coming months. (Fain family.)

Ranchers no doubt made a profit from the sale of their cattle, but here a hungry calf and two lambs are "making a profit," as this picture has been named. (Fain family.)

The ranchers were also farmers, as they grew their fields of hay and barley to provide for winter feed for their herds. Here workers harvest the grain for future use. (Fain family.)

Breaking horses was another task for the cowboy. Here several cowboys restrain a horse while a rider gets ready to mount. (Fain family.)

The Fain ranch house in Lonesome Valley appears to be a rather lonesome spread against the background of a wide-open valley. (Fain family.)

Dan Fain astride his horse was a familiar sight. As stated in Dean Smith's book *The Fains of Lonesome Valley*, "Any life style that did not include rising before dawn and riding out on the range to work was not for him." (Fain family.)

Ranching has been a tradition in the Fain family since William and Cary Fain first arrived in Arizona in 1874. Granville, better known as Dan, was born in 1879 in Cornville, Arizona. He is pictured here on the right with his son Norman and grandson Bill. (Fain family.)

Not to be forgotten are the ranch families who carry on family life during the hectic ranch activities. Johnie Lee Fain and two of her children are seen here appearing none the worse for wear. Johnie Lee not only attended to her duties as housewife but also helped out on the ranch when needed. (Fain family.)

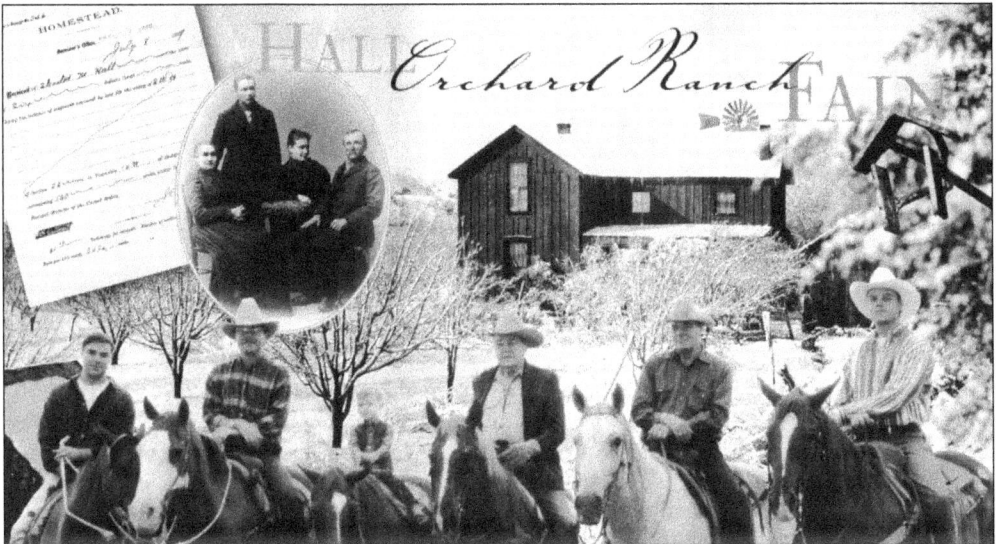

This postcard shows two of Lonesome Valley's prominent ranch families. Generations of the Fain family are pictured at the bottom, while Sharlot Hall's family and home at Orchard Ranch appear across the top. (Fain family.)

The Hall family arrived in 1872 and settled along Lynx Creek near their relatives the Bobletts. James Hall engaged in mining along the creek and later acquired a homestead farther down the creek. The ranch was called Orchard Ranch and today is a mobile home park of the same name. Sharlot was expected to take part in many of the ranch chores, even feeding piglets, as seen here. Sharlot was of a sensitive nature, and though she had very little formal education, she was renowned for her talent as a writer and poetess. She was the first woman appointed state historian in Arizona and traveled extensively throughout the territory to acquaint herself with the history of Arizona. All this was done while attending to her duties on the ranch. Eventually she moved into Prescott and founded the Sharlot Hall Museum. (Fain family.)

Four

TRAILS AND TRACKS

As the population of Arizona increased, so did the need for supplies. Merchants wanted additional merchandise, ranchers and miners needed equipment and a means to transport their products, and newcomers required a means to carry their belongings. The business of transporting goods to and from the territory for some proved to be a profitable enterprise.

Trails were becoming established as goods were shipped via the Gulf of California and the Colorado River. Ehrenberg became a port of entry into the new territory. A trail from there, the Ehrenberg Road, served to transport goods to Wickenburg and Prescott. As this trail traversed an arid country, stage stops with their wells became welcome sights as freighters and stagecoaches wended their way into the interior.

Farther up the river, Thomas Hardy founded the town of Hardyville. His trail followed through mountains and valleys on its way to Prescott. Both these routes were fraught with danger from marauding bands and deplorable conditions, but they served to transport the necessities of life to the new settlers.

When the territorial capital was moved to Tucson in 1867, communication among Prescott, the newly founded town of Phoenix, and the capital became necessary. It was soon determined that a trail connecting these towns was needed. Thus the Black Canyon Highway was constructed to transport stagecoaches and supplies. This road passed through Lonesome Valley, Dewey, Humboldt, and Mayer. The mines in the Bradshaw Mountains also made use of this route.

But trails proved to be not only dangerous but also very slow and arduous. In 1897, Frank Murphy started construction of the Prescott and Eastern Railroad to serve part of the route. The railroad branched off from the Peavine Railroad in Granite Dells, running southeast through Lonesome Valley.

Paved four-lane highways cover these routes today. Stage stops have been replaced by motels, gas stations, and fast food restaurants. Cars, buses, and trucks cover the distances in hours that once took days.

As the new territory became more populated, supplies were transported to ports on the Colorado River and then loaded on to freight wagons to be delivered to Prescott. These ruts are still visible along the Hardyville Trail. Tufa, which is a rather porous material, shows the wear of the wagon wheels that once traversed the trail with heavy loads. (Nigel Reynolds.)

In some cases, it was necessary to remove rocks along the trail. They were placed along the edge of the trail, which helped to identify the route and made for a smoother ride. (Nigel Reynolds.)

Rocks were also used to stabilize the trail through low-lying areas and along precipitous routes. Creating such trails was labor-intensive work, and it was done by the freighters themselves. (Nigel Reynolds.)

In 1998, a Historic Trail group was formed as a result of a Historic Trails Conference held in Prescott. This group has concentrated on the old trails within Yavapai County. In identifying the routes, they look for artifacts such as this tin can to help them trace the road and the campsites frequented by the freighters. (Nigel Reynolds.)

Other artifacts are also found along the trail. Mule shoes as well as horseshoes, bottles, and wagon parts are carefully analyzed to determine their authenticity and age. (Nigel Reynolds.)

Travel along these trails was fraught with danger. Marauding bands were bent on attacking wagon trains and stagecoaches. Weather was often a hindrance, as roads became rutted in rain and snow. Falls, injuries, and sickness presented other problems, and the environment held its dangers, such as this rattlesnake ready to strike its prey. (Nigel Reynolds.)

Wild animals were also encountered in the wilderness. This cougar seems to be ready to pounce upon an unwary traveler. Such animals still prowl the mountains and canyons today. (Stew Schrauger/ Natural Visions Photography.)

The Old Black Canyon Highway became the preferred route between Prescott and Phoenix by the late 1870s. It shortened the previous trip by way of Wickenburg by several days. This sign at the corner of Highways 69 and 169 identifies the route as it passed through Dewey, Arizona. (Author collection.)

This road parallels Highway 69 as it passes the former Young's Farm. It was once part of the Old Black Canyon Highway on its way to Humboldt and Mayer. From that point, it began its precipitous descent though the Black Canyon. (Author collection.)

The trail seen here passes through the FX Ranch on its way to Mayer, Arizona. Rough road conditions and uncomfortable wagons were not the only hazards for travelers. Bands of highwaymen often attacked the wagons. (Author collection.)

This wagon on exhibit in Humboldt, Arizona, is reminiscent of the means of conveyance in the 19th-century Arizona Territory. Such a wagon may have carried passengers along the road to Phoenix. (Author collection.)

Transportation in the territory did improve somewhat with the arrival of the railroad. This sign at the entrance of today's Rails to Trails in Prescott explains the urgency for better transportation. The Prescott and Arizona Central Railroad answered that need. (Darcy Morger Grovenstein.)

In 1897, Frank Murphy saw the possibility of constructing a railroad through Lonesome Valley to Mayer and thence to Crown King. This railroad would serve not only the ranches but also the miners. The road began in Granite Dells, where it branched off from the Peavine Railroad. The junction of these roads is shown here. (Sharlot Hall Museum.)

Once the Prescott and Eastern Railroad reached Mayer, Murphy continued construction of the Bradshaw Railroad to Crown King. As laborers were in short supply, jail inmates were given the choice of a jail cell or work on the railroad. (Sharlot Hall Museum.)

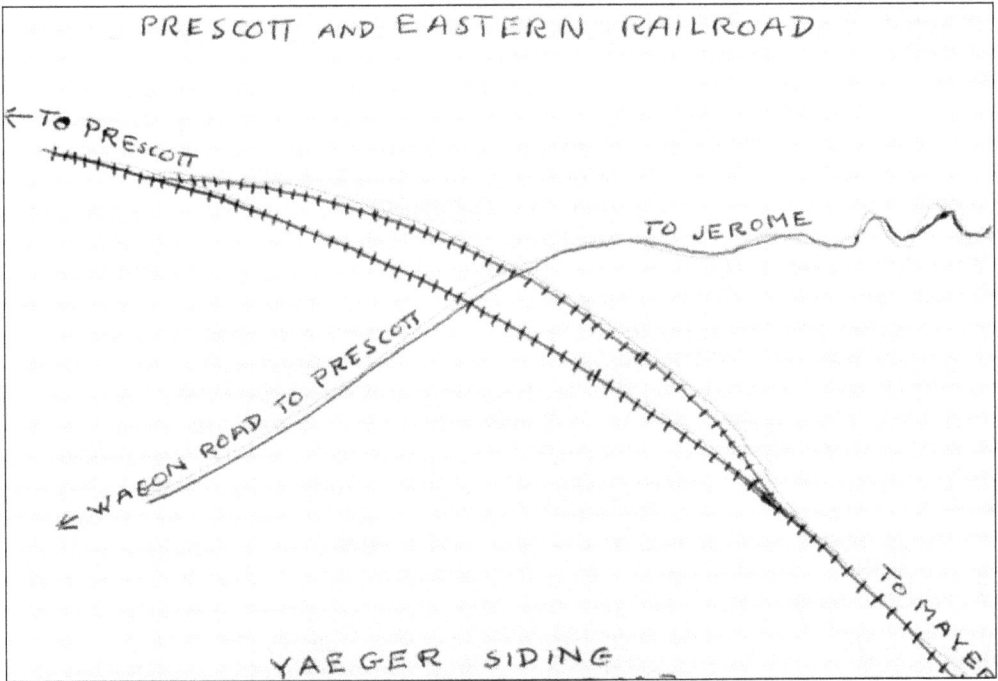

PRESCOTT AND EASTERN RAILROAD

←TO PRESCOTT

TO JEROME

←WAGON ROAD TO PRESCOTT

TO MAYER

YAEGER SIDING

Sidings such as this one in Lonesome Valley at the entrance to Yaeger Canyon provided access to ranchers and miners. Thomas Sanders used this siding to unload supplies, which he then freighted across the mountain to Jerome. (Author collection.)

The Prescott and Eastern Railroad continued to be in use well into the 20th century. When the rails were removed, the rail bed was converted to a trail and named the Iron King Trail. (Author collection.)

The Iron King Trail enters Granite Dells at the western edge of Prescott Valley. It once was the rail bed of the Prescott and Eastern Railroad. (Darcy Morger Grovenstein.)

To add to the significance of the Iron King Trail as a former railroad, old equipment has been placed along the trail. It would appear that such equipment also provides a place to catch one's breath and take a rest while hiking this picturesque trail. (Darcy Morger Grovenstein.)

Five

THE RISE OF A TOWN

As a teenager, Bill Fain proved to be a prophet when he proclaimed, "Someday this valley will have more people than Prescott." Highway 69 had just been completed from Interstate 17 to Prescott and passed through Lonesome Valley. It opened up that area to possible urban development.

It was not long before that possibility became a reality. In 1964, Ned Warren, the self-proclaimed "Godfather of Arizona land schemes," approached Norman Fain with one of these schemes. Ned proposed a development in Lonesome Valley. After initiating negotiations, Ned left for Kingman to engage in a similar deal and placed the company in the hands of Robert Loos and Leonard Hoffman. These two formed Prescott Valley, Inc., and began peddling property across the country.

Promising "You'll Live in the Sun in Prescott Valley," Prescott Valley, Inc., took its message to the midwest and northeastern states. They offered a steak dinner and showed pictures of Prescott, the national forest, area lakes, and ranches. They were able to convince attendees to purchase property sight unseen, and sales were fairly brisk.

Property owners were invited to visit the new community to view their purchase. A motel and dining room were built to accommodate these visitors. They were also treated to a tour of the surrounding points of interest. Upon viewing their property, dissatisfied owners were given the options of trading their lot for a more desirable location or receiving a return of their payments. In some instances, these visitors not only approved of their purchase but bought additional lots. Prescott Valley, Inc., and its staff were intent on satisfying the needs of their new residents and realized that the new development was rather remote and devoid of needed necessities of life. They therefore began a rather vigorous building campaign with the addition of a gas station, activity building, and a strip mall. Roads were graded and some infrastructure provided for the new community.

The first post office in Prescott Valley was opened in 1969. The building that housed it was originally a tack room at the stables. It was moved to the southwest corner of Robert Road across from the sales office for Prescott Valley, Inc., at the main entrance to the town. (*Fringe Benefit.*)

Pictured here is Prescott Valley's first postmaster, Christie A. Hansen, accompanied by his wife, Maxine (center), and Shirley Sellers. The Hansens moved to Prescott Valley from Spencer, Iowa, where he served as postmaster for 33 years. (*Fringe Benefit.*)

As can be seen from this February 1, 1969, first cancellation, the postmark shows the post office location as Agua Fria, Arizona, while the First Day Cancellation stamp records the name as Prescott Valley. One explanation according to the January 1969 *Fringe Benefit* states that the "station will serve the entire Agua Fria Valley," of which Prescott Valley is a part. (*Fringe Benefit.*)

This unpretentious-looking building was once the first post office and library. Shelves were placed in a corner of the room and lined with books purchased by Prescott Valley, Inc., to become the town's first library. (*Fringe Benefit.*)

Three years after the founding of Prescott Valley, the area caught the eye of Republic International Motion Picture Corporation. This company saw fit to film its version of *Mountain Men* in 1969 in Prescott Valley. Even some of the newly arrived residents served as extras along with the company's cowboys, Indians, and good and bad guys. (*Fringe Benefit.*)

This fort was a prop in the shooting of the *Mountain Men* movie. It was later moved to the park area and named "Old Fort Laramie." The fort served as a new prop for the young people of Prescott Valley. (*Fringe Benefit.*)

To carry out the Western theme of the new community, Prescott Valley, Inc., acquired a cow named Agatha. Agatha must have been in a "family way," as she soon gave birth to Li'l Cowhyde Clyde—a handsome bull. Clyde became the first official resident of Prescott Valley's newly constructed barn. (*Fringe Benefit.*)

In an effort to present Prescott Valley as an established community and an attractive place to call home, the company began to spruce up the entrance with this nicely landscaped island to greet visitors as they turned off the highway. (*Fringe Benefit.*)

Prescott Valley, Inc., felt the need to keep new and prospective residents informed of the progress of the new community. Copies of the *Fringe Benefit* were sent out each month recording the arrival of property owners, the construction of facilities, and activities being enjoyed by the residents. The name "Fringe Benefit" denoted that this was just another fringe benefit provided by the company. (*Fringe Benefit.*)

Another fringe benefit provided by the company was an activity building. Since it was an A-frame type of construction, it became known as the A Frame. Residents were encouraged to hold activities such as potluck suppers, club meetings, game nights, and, as seen here, church services. Rev. Robert Cooley came from Prescott each Sunday morning to conduct services. (*Fringe Benefit.*)

The company realized Prescott Valley was a distance from the nearest shopping area, so it began providing some of the necessities for the residents. One of the first of these was a gas station. It was offered to any resident looking for a business opportunity. Lon Stevenson became the owner and opened a Richfield station in 1969. (*Fringe Benefit.*)

This picture had the caption "Fill 'Er Up," and that is just what Little Buck is doing. It was thought that another pump should be added labeled "pasteurized." (*Fringe Benefit.*)

Another fringe benefit was the addition of a motel, named the Prescott Valley Motel. This facility was built to provide accommodations to property owners when they came to view their property. They were invited to stay in the motel as guests of the company. After viewing their property, if dissatisfied with the location, they were offered the option to trade for another lot or a refund of their payments. Several bought additional properties. Here the Schaffers from Minnesota arrive at their room at the motel. (*Fringe Benefit.*)

While visiting the area, property owners were made comfortable in the motel and fed in the adjacent Coffee Shop. New residents were given the opportunity to find employment in these facilities. Here Barbara Copeland arrives at work at the new restaurant. (*Fringe Benefit.*)

In an effort to continue to supply the new community with needed supplies, Prescott Valley, Inc., began the construction of a strip mall along Highway 69. The first store to open was a grocery store. A new resident, Al Cox, is shown here unloading the first shipment of groceries for the Prescott Valley Market. (*Fringe Benefit.*)

The arrival of a delivery truck at the store was a big event, since it meant residents could stock their pantries by simply driving "up front," as the new mall was becoming known. (*Fringe Benefit.*)

As the year 1969 drew to a close, Robert Loos (left), president of Prescott Valley, Inc., and Leonard Hoffman (below), chairman of the board, recorded their enthusiasm for the growing community and their appreciation of the spirit of the residents. In the Christmas newsletter, they expressed their thanks to the residents by saying, "As the year 1969 draws to a close, we are able to reflect upon its passing with a genuine sense of achievement. The support and enthusiasm of our fine Prescott Valley family greatly accelerated our original plans for expansion and advancement." (Both, *Fringe Benefit*.)

Dale Copeland and daughter Robyn ride into the sunset as the year 1969 draws to a close. It was a year that saw the construction of much-needed facilities, such as the A Frame, the gas station, and the grocery store. It also gave promise of more to come in the future. Prescott Valley was beginning to take on the appearance of a town. (*Fringe Benefit.*)

Although this mobile home appears well established in this 1970 photograph, these two ladies, Evelyn Myers (left) and her sister Vida Anderson, arrived in the area in 1967. They were the valley's first residents, and they spent their first night alone in what had been known as Lonesome Valley. It must have seemed lonesome indeed. (*Fringe Benefit.*)

Even in the mid-1970s, Prescott Valley was a rather lonesome place. The area shown here is south of today's Lakeshore Drive. With the construction of the lakes and Lake Shore Drive, Warren Road, named for the man who first recognized Lonesome Valley as a location for one of his land deals, was shortened and the remainder of the road renamed. (Jeffries family.)

Evelyn and Vida were soon joined by an unusual couple on Jay Court, Myrtle and Gerry Kirwin, better known as Kookie and Beans in "clowning circles." The Kirwins hailed from Massachusetts and moved west after their son contracted rheumatic fever. As members of the Phoenix Clown Club and Clowns International, Kookie and Beans have played clowns for love not money, bringing joy to thousands in hospitals and for other charitable causes. (*Fringe Benefit.*)

This scene became a familiar one as new residents arrived to take possession of their property. Many were accommodated in the Prescott Valley Motel until they could acquire more permanent living arrangements. (*Fringe Benefit*.)

In some cases, Prescott Valley, Inc., hosted bus trips to Arizona. Pictured here is a group from Des Moines, Iowa, traveling to Prescott Valley to view their property, which they had purchased sight unseen. (*Fringe Benefit*.)

The A Frame proved to be a gathering place on many occasions. Prescott Valley, Inc., donated a Kimball organ to be used at church services. Mrs. Calvin Schultz (Marjory) became the organist, and according to the newsletter, the organ "proved to be a highly attractive, invaluable addition to our Sunday services." (*Fringe Benefit.*)

In 1969, David Sellers was the only student boarding the school bus to be taken to attend high school in Prescott. The number continued to increase throughout the years. Elementary school students attended school in Humboldt. (*Fringe Benefit.*)

At the end of that school year, 14 children were transported home to the valley to begin their summer vacation. (*Fringe Benefit.*)

This picture is titled "Fashionable Winter Garb in Prescott Valley" in the newsletter and depicts a bricklayer working on the completion of the strip mall. Since it was taken in February 1970 at a temperature of 70 degrees, Midwesterners could add this to the many reasons for their move to Arizona. (*Fringe Benefit.*)

By the spring of 1970, the strip mall at the entrance to Prescott Valley was complete and ready for occupancy. It was not long before shops opened to provide more of the necessities for the residents. (*Fringe Benefit.*)

Residents began thinking of ways to supplement their income while providing needed services to the new community. Darlene Gahms opened a beauty salon next to the Laundromat. She is seen here entering her new business on opening day. (*Fringe Benefit.*)

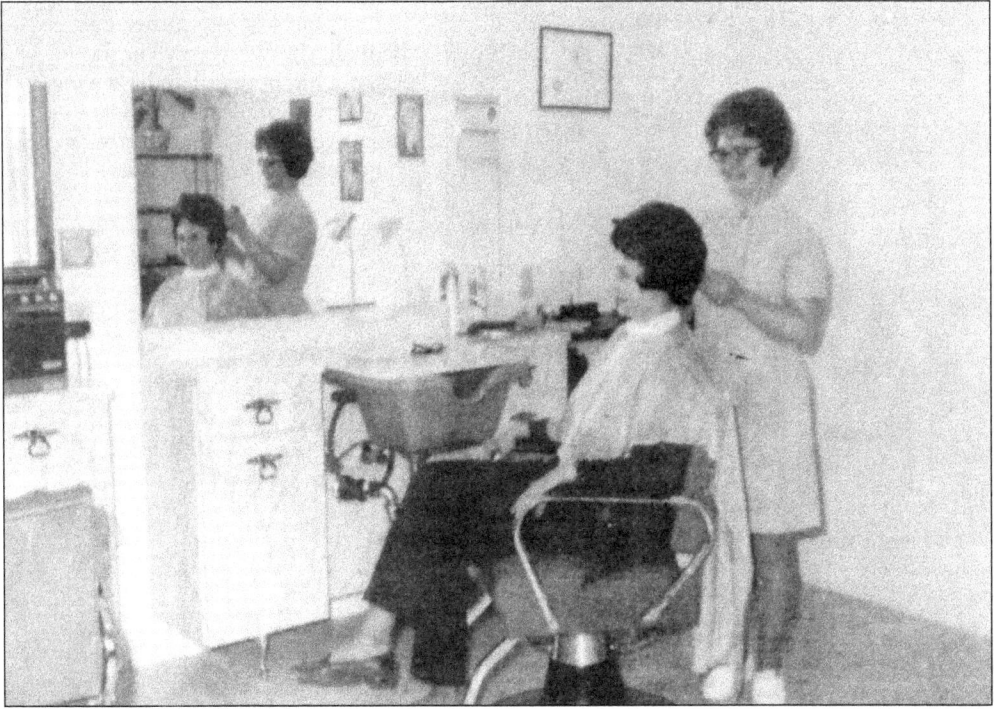

A "Grand Opening Special" was offered to the first patrons of the beauty salon. Darlene gave a discount of $3 to her first customers. (*Fringe Benefit.*)

The *Fringe Benefit* kept property owners informed of the latest developments in Prescott Valley. One of the featured articles appearing in each issue was written by a resident, Shirley Sellers. Her articles were filled with news of new arrivals, community activities, and pictures of recent business openings. Shirley often organized activities in the A Frame to bring people together to become better acquainted. Her family arrived in 1968 and located their mobile home on Romero Circle. Her husband, Rolly, worked in the sales office of Prescott Valley, Inc. (*Fringe Benefit.*)

To carry out a Western theme in the mall, the Western Wear shop placed a hitching rail and watering trough in front of the store for the convenience of those arriving on horseback. (Sandra Sasser.)

In 1971, another building was added to the west end of the mall. It was to house a branch of the Great Western Bank. This business was indeed a welcome addition to the new town, as residents could now carry on their business locally instead of making the trip into Prescott. Steve Campbell was the first branch manager. (*Fringe Benefit*.)

This aerial view of what was once Lonesome Valley shows the progress made within a few years. The motel, the gas station, the A Frame, and the park are seen here together with the strip mall, sales office, and post office. These comprised the business section of the town along Highway 69. Some apartments can also be seen in the background. (*Fringe Benefit.*)

Reminders of the past occupants can be seen here as they graze across the fence of one of the first homes to occupy the valley. Wildlife such as pronghorn, deer, javelinas, coyotes, and rabbits continued to live in the area and sometimes in the yards of the residents. Here some friendly cattle are visiting their new neighbors. (*Fringe Benefit.*)

Pronghorn were frequent visitors in the valley. This picture taken in 1989 shows their presence near the civic center as they grazed peacefully close to the new community. It became necessary to relocate these animals as development began to occupy their grazing land. (Stew Schrauger/ Natural Visions Photography.)

Travel in the new town left much to be desired, especially during stormy weather. Since the area does receive some snow during the winter months, travel was particularly difficult at that time. Roads were graded but not paved until later and then only the main streets. Cars were often seen covered with mud as residents made their way along the rutted streets. (*Fringe Benefit.*)

This picture, titled "What's Winter, Mommy," further accentuates the pleasures enjoyed in the balmy weather in Prescott Valley. The pool was another benefit provided by Prescott Valley, Inc., and was located behind the Prescott Valley Motel. (*Fringe Benefit.*)

However, Prescott Valley does have winter, as can be seen here. In fact, in 1967, the area received several feet of snow. This picture was taken in 1977, so Prescott Valley does get its share of the white stuff. (Jeffries family.)

Leonard Hoffman, chairman of the board, is seen here on the left as he points to plans for the new corporate office in Phoenix. From left to right, Pres. Robert Loos, Vice Pres. Clyde Dinnell, and company director J. Kelly Farris look on. (*Fringe Benefit.*)

By 1970, Prescott Valley, Inc., had outgrown its original office. In May 1970, plans were underway to move to 300 East Camelback Road in Phoenix. The executives of the company declared that "Business is Booming" and "surpassing all original hopes and dreams." Ten thousand lots had been sold in the first seven to eight years. (*Fringe Benefit.*)

Most visitors to Prescott Valley arrived by car, but the Petersons arrived from Cambridge, Minnesota, via their motorcycle and pulling a trailer. They look none the worse for wear after their long trip and happy to be at the end of their journey. (*Fringe Benefit.*)

Another fringe benefit provided by Prescott Valley, Inc., was a lake called Lake Yavapai. A wash area was dammed up to form the lake. It was stocked with fish and fitted out with a dock and rowboats ready for Prescott Valley fishermen. It has also been reported that there was a 28-foot houseboat provided for those who suffered from seasickness. (*Fringe Benefit.*)

Realizing that as the population of the town increased security was becoming more necessary, Prescott Valley, Inc., hired the Roadrunner Security Patrol. Three agents were assigned to patrol the area, and the residents slept better at night knowing protection was at hand. Prescott Valley, Inc., also donated land and a building to house fire equipment. (*Fringe Benefit.*)

An air strip was built along Route 69 east of Truwood Drive to serve as Prescott Valley's "airport." Here Mrs. Clyde Dinnell flew in from Phoenix with what looks like supplies for the Dinnell pantry. (*Fringe Benefit.*)

Another addition to the community in 1970 was the Valley Hut. The Wegges were kept busy serving up soda, sandwiches, chicken and shrimp in a basket, and ice cream. (*Fringe Benefit*.)

What else does a growing community need? A good restaurant would be nice. In 1970, Buster and Marian Duzan saw such a need and began construction of the Coachlight Inn. A relaxed and comfortable atmosphere was enjoyed by diners in the Western-style dining room complete with fireplace and crackling fire. The lounge area also followed a Western motif and was called the Tom a Hawk Lounge. A hitching post in the parking lot was provided for those who arrived on a four-legged conveyance. (*Fringe Benefit*.)

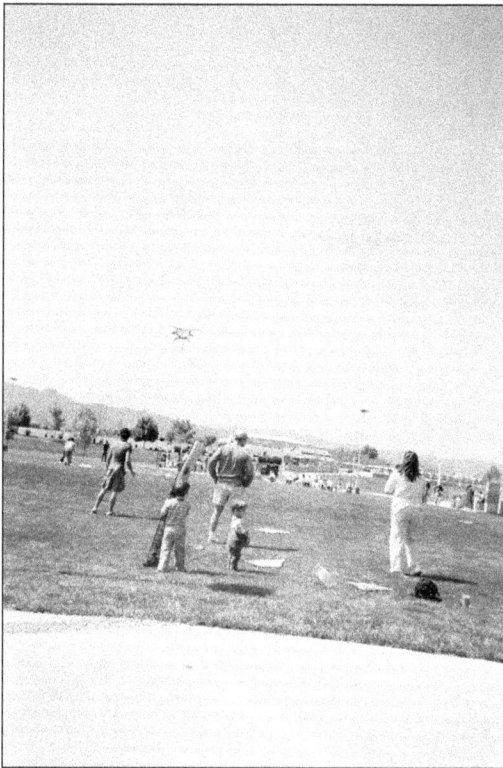

With the spring winds in the valley, kite flying has always been a popular activity. Early inhabitants engaged in this sport, and even 40 years later, the town offers competitions, as seen here. Kite flyers assembled at the civic center to engage in such a competition in 2008. (Author collection.)

Once school closed for the summer, the youngsters headed for the pool behind the motel. It looks like they are also enjoying another fringe benefit as they paddle miniature canoes. The roof of the A Frame is visible behind the fence surrounding the pool. (*Fringe Benefit.*)

The A Frame was the scene of many community activities. Margo Stevenson directed a ceramics class for children held each Saturday morning. One was also held for adults during the week. (*Fringe Benefit.*)

Holidays were celebrated with great enthusiasm. Here children are dressed in Halloween costumes on their way to go trick-or-treating. (*Fringe Benefit.*)

Glassford Hill is Prescott Valley's landmark. It was once called Bald Mountain or Mount Baldy. The name was changed in honor of Col. William A. Glassford, who established a heliograph station on the hill in the 1890s. These two young hikers climbed the hill to visit this historic site. (*Fringe Benefit.*)

In keeping with the spirit of the West, some young fellows organized a group called the Valley Plainsmen. Their goal was to reenact scenes of the Old West by participating in celebrations. They engaged in mock hangings, poker games, and incarcerating "criminals" in their jail during Prescott Valley Days. They also entered their float in parades and staged Old West scenes wearing frontiersman costumes. (*Fringe Benefit.*)

A
♠

Your Presence is
Requested to
Witness

HANGINGS   SHOOT-OUTS

THE
VALLEY
PLAINSMEN

OLD WEST PORTRAYALS

P.O. Box 25833
Prescott Valley, Arizona 86312

♥
A

One reason for the move to the Southwest was the leisurely lifestyle and the great outdoors. From left to right, Franchon, Verle, and Tommy Jeffries take advantage of a sunny day to take a ride on their horses. (*Fringe Benefit.*)

The fort used in the movie *Mountain Men* was moved to the park and was often the scene of gatherings such as this "council fire." A marshmallow roast started off the event. (*Fringe Benefit.*)

Visitors to Prescott Valley interested in the history of the area ventured down a dirt road to view a house built in 1890 by a miner named Thomas Gibson Barlow Massicks. This man carried on a very successful mining operation along Lynx Creek until his untimely death in 1899 from an accidental bullet wound. (*Fringe Benefit.*)

It was gold that brought the early settlers to the area, and mining is still carried on by such hopeful miners as this modern-day gold panner. (Author collection.)

As the population increased and more families arrived, the education of the children became a concern. In the fall of 1972, Lake Valley Elementary School opened in Prescott Valley to admit kindergarten through third-grade students. (Darcy Morger Grovenstein.)

In 1976, plans for a new high school were formulated, and ground-breaking took place on January 27. The school was located midway between Prescott Valley and Humboldt. It accommodated grade 7 through 12. Opening day was in the fall of 1977. (Author collection.)

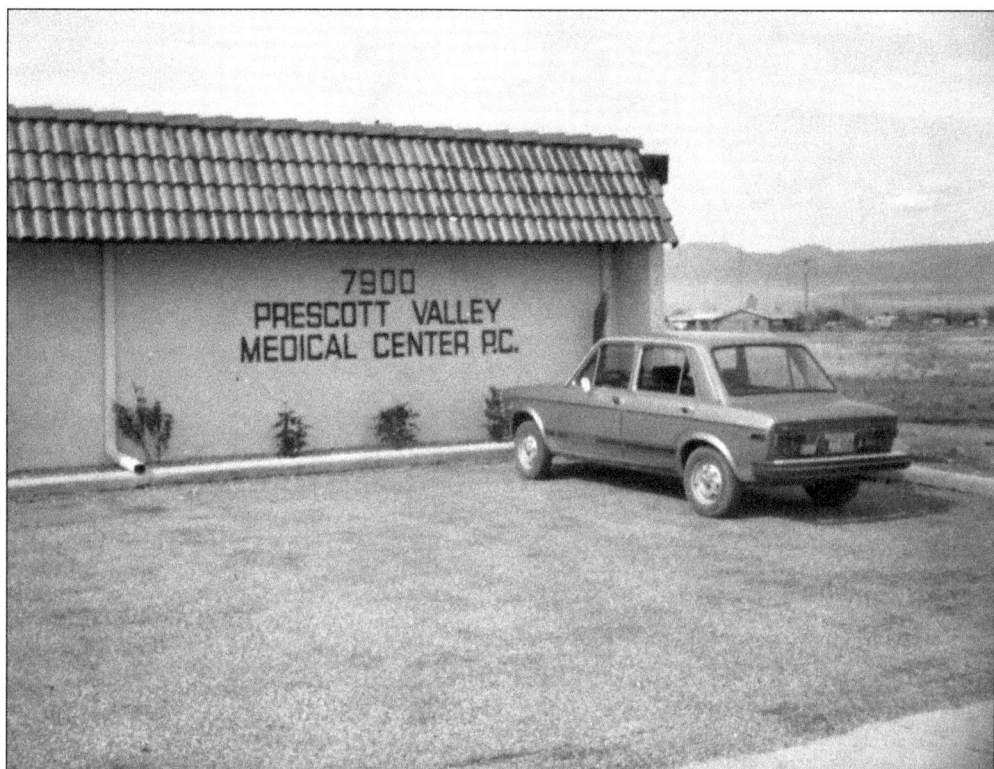

Health care also became a concern for early residents. The nearest doctors and hospital were 8 miles away in Prescott. A health center opened in the valley in the mid-1970s. (Dorothy Roberts.)

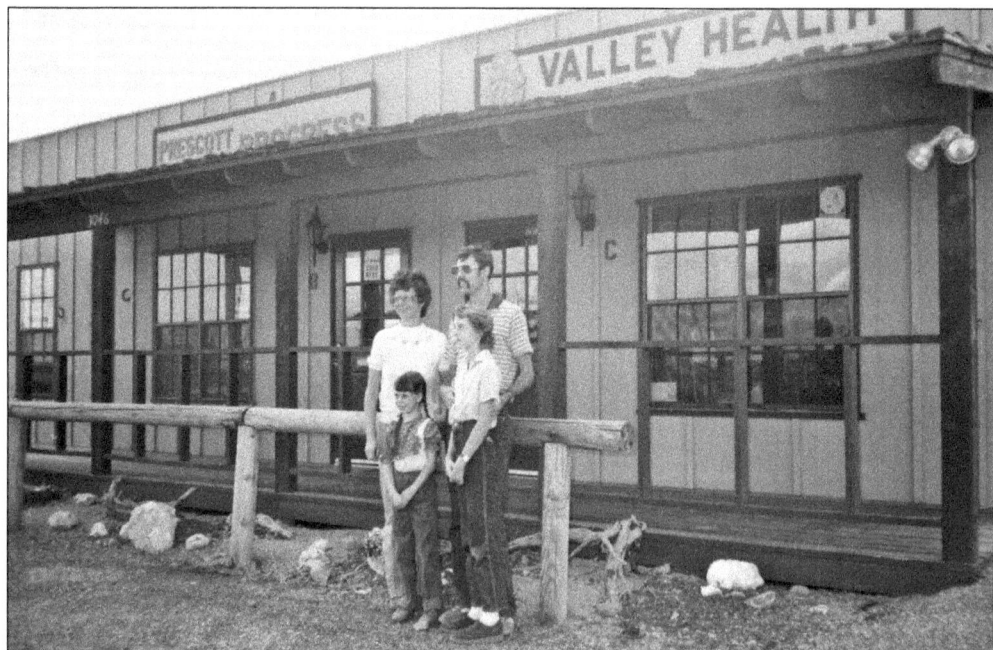

Prescott Valley had its own newspaper after the incorporation of the town. About 1980, the Robertses began publishing the *Prescott Valley Tribune*. (Dorothy Roberts.)

Residents continued to move into the valley, and some purchased additional properties as investment real estate. Prescott Valley was on its way to becoming a town. (*Fringe Benefit.*)

Realizing that the Arizona sun could be utilized in producing energy, Solar Plumbing and Electrical Company opened this business on Valley Road. It was co-owned by Dennis Vons and Curtis Bonnelli. In keeping with its name, the building had a south-facing glass facade. (*Fringe Benefit.*)

Dennis Voss and Curtis Bonelli, co-owners of the Solar Plumbing Electrical Contracting Company are rightfully proud of their functional and innovative building recently completed at 2230 Valley Road.

Prescott Valley was flying high and on its way to becoming an incorporated town. The balloon festivals held in the 1980s seemed to personify the growth of the new community, as it had taken off from its humble beginnings to soar into the future as a vital, growing community. (*Fringe Benefit.*)

Six

INCORPORATION

From its very beginning, Prescott Valley residents saw the necessity of forming a community association. It was not long before it was deemed advisable to consider incorporation for the growing community. In 1973, a committee was formed to explore the possibility of incorporation for the new town. This committee labored tirelessly for the next five years in securing such a status.

According to Arizona law, any incorporated community within 6 miles of a proposed town must vote approval of the incorporation of that town. Prescott Valley petitioned the City of Prescott to approve the proposed incorporation. This was accomplished on May 8, 1978, when a resolution was passed to allow Prescott Valley to hold an election seeking incorporation. The resolution passed with a 5-2 vote.

The next step in the process required the town to petition the Yavapai County Board of Supervisors to call for a general election. August 22, 1978, was selected as the date for this election. If approved by the voters, the county would declare the community of Prescott Valley an incorporated town.

Following a successful election, the Prescott Valley Community Association submitted a list of names from which seven were selected by the county board to comprise the first town council. The council in turn selected the mayor. This council served until the first general election, which was held on May 15, 1979.

To celebrate this momentous occasion, the town organized its first Prescott Valley Days celebration complete with a parade, games, food, and a mock hanging by the Lonesome Valley Plainsmen. Attendees not clad in Western wear were jailed. An evening dance concluded the festivities.

Thus Prescott Valley became an incorporated town and was no longer dependent on Prescott Valley, Inc. It was now ready to launch out on its own. A new town hall was built on Cochise Drive to serve as the town's offices and council chambers.

Along with this new sign erected by the chamber of commerce welcoming visitors to Prescott Valley, the town took on a new image in 1978. Twelve years after the beginning of the development by Prescott Valley, Inc., the residents were ready to launch out on their own and become Prescott Valley—an incorporated town. They were ready to vote to make this possible. (*Fringe Benefit.*)

August 22, 1978, was the date selected for residents to cast their votes and make the incorporation a reality. Voters flocked to the polls, and a total of 80 percent of the residents lined up to record their vote. From left to right, Pat Hansen, Marietta McFadden, Mildred Nelson, and Harold Phillips were among the volunteers at the polling place. (*Fringe Benefit.*)

By 1 o'clock on election day, ballot count indicated that it would be a record turnout as residents came in by twos, by threes and singly to have their say as to the future of their community. And, when the last ballot was tallied and the corresponding cut stubs matched in count, it was official ... **Prescott Valley was a city**, a town, a registered member of the important Arizona Cities and Towns ... and a new page in history had been written.

The official mailing address for anyone in Prescott Valley is: Name, address (or P.O. Box number), Agua Fria Rural Branch Prescott, AZ 86312.

With 80% turnout, residents came alone and in groups, waiting in line when necessary to cast their vote.

Residents lined up to vote for incorporation. A total of 80 percent of the residents cast their ballots in this election. (*Fringe Benefit.*)

Volunteers Gary Moran (left) and Anton Schager manned the ballot box. Stubs were cut off of the ballots before they were inserted into the ballot box. At the end of the day, a tally of ballots and stubs was taken and matched. (*Fringe Benefit.*)

With the incorporation of Prescott Valley a reality, an interim council was appointed by the county. In May 1979, the town held its first general election to elect members of the town council, which included Mayor Richard Addis and Vice Mayor Marilyn Horne. (Both, *Fringe Benefit*.)

VOLUME 10, NUMBER 12   A PRESCOTT VALLEY, INCORPORATED PUBLICATION   JULY, 1979

P. V. Residents Elect First Town Council

| MAYOR RICHARD ADDIS | VICE MAYOR MARILYN HORNE | CHARLIE ROBINSON | RAYMOND SANDBERG | ART KING | PAUL POLLARD | RICHARD McGINNIS |

Other members of the council appointed by the county were Charlie Robinson, Raymond Sandberg, Art King, Paul Pollard, and Richard McGinnis. Prescott Valley was now ready to set off on its own as an incorporated community. (*Fringe Benefit*.)

90

To celebrate the incorporation of Prescott Valley, the town organized the First Annual Prescott Valley Days. The festivities included a parade, games, food, and a dance. Prizes were awarded for different categories of floats in the parade. Residents lined Main Street as the parade wended its way along. This antique car was one of the parade entrants. (*Fringe Benefit.*)

During the celebration, the Valley Plainsmen had to get into the act. They staged a robbery at high noon. After capturing the robber, they led him to the jail to serve his sentence. (*Fringe Benefit.*)

With the opening of the new community center on Manzanita Circle, the A Frame also took on a new life and opened as the Bar-B-Q restaurant. Later it became a Mexican restaurant called Glendito's. (*Fringe Benefit*.)

Wearing A New Look

A special treat for holiday shoppers and folks on the go is the recent opening of the P.V. Bar-B-Que Restaurant located in the A-Frame building, a familiar and favorite P.V. landmark.

Featuring yummy bar-b-que beef, pork, ribs and chili with hot bread and cole slaw, the new eatery is owned by Bernie Fisher of Prescott and is being operated by two of the eight Fisher children, Bob and Lisa.

With a mother from Texas, it was a natural to borrow her tried and true down home recipes and the Fishers have combined tasty treats with a warm and informal atmosphere featuring a pool table and a jukebox for dancing. A huge steam boiler from an old mine dominates the main floor and provides heat and the bar-b-que cookery. The upstairs loft, as well as the main floor, has comfortable picnic tables for eating and casual visiting. Open from 11 A.M. until 9 P.M., the P.V. Bar-B-Que serves lunch, dinner and snacks every day except Wednesday.

Today the A Frame is another Mexican restaurant called Oliva's. The restaurant has been enlarged by the addition of another A-frame to accommodate more seating and a lounge area. (*Fringe Benefit*.)

VOLUME 9, NUMBER 7   A PRESCOTT VALLEY, INCORPORATED PUBLICATION

New Market Is Safeway's Largest In The State

PRESCOTT VALLEY SALUTES SAFEWA

reading and greeting card center.

Open seven days a week, the store will employ more than 40 people from the area and is predicted by the Safeway regional office in Phoenix to become one of the most successful and profitable store in the state within the next two to three years.

The Safeway chain extends across the country, into Canada and 13 European countries and is the biggest sales and dollar profit market in the world. With the largest sales volume of any grocery store in Arizona, Safeway chose the Prescott Valley location because of the residential growth potential of the area and a basic need now, and particularly in the near future, for a large modern supermarket, determined by their own extensive marketing studies.

Revco Drug and Sprouse-Reitz Variety are expected to open within the month and Westcor, Incorporated of Phoenix, developer and builder of the entire P.V. Plaza Shopping Center, have additional plans for other smaller shops and a restaurant.

specials, free hot dogs, cokes, balloons, lollipops and favors to all who passed through the electonic portals. Drawings

Another momentous development in 1978 was the opening of the Safeway Plaza. This shopping mall was located across the highway from the strip mall. Revco Drug Store, Sprouse Ritz, and Yellow Front also located in the plaza. Prescott Valley was launched into a new era as it not only became a town but also began to look like one, too. (*Fringe Benefit.*)

Seven

PRESENT-DAY PRESCOTT VALLEY

Forty one years ago, two sisters, Evelyn Myers and Vida Anderson, spent their first night in Prescott Valley all alone. It was 1967 and the development was just one year old. These two pioneer ladies had moved their mobile home to Unit 3 on Jay Court. Lonesome Valley must have seemed lonesome indeed.

In just 42 years, the fledgling community has increased in population until today more than 35,000 people call Prescott Valley home. At an elevation of 5,100 feet, the region provides a mild four-season climate for those wishing to escape the severe winters of the midwest and the extreme heat of the southern states.

Lured here by the enterprising founders of the community, many of the early citizens endured the inconveniences of dirt roads and lack of utilities and other necessary facilities to create the vibrant community it is today. The founders of the development were well aware of the lack of facilities and began at once to furnish some of the basic necessities.

Others must have recognized the desirability of the area. A U.S. Post Office opened in 1969, and a movie company chose this area to film their version of *Mountain Men*. Safeway Plaza was built in 1978. Better Built Aluminum and Print Pack followed a few years later. Since then, Lockheed Martin, Superior Industries, Ace Hardware Retail Support Center, and numerous smaller businesses have located in the area. Banks, motels, retail stores, and restaurants have found this location to their liking. A new entertainment district, a sports arena, and the relocated county fair buildings provide pastime amusements. Churches, schools, and parks are also available. Prescott Valley has come a long way in 40 years from a Lonesome Valley to the bustling town of the 21st century.

"Live in the sun in Prescott Valley" was a slogan used by the early developers in advertising material as they peddled their properties across the country. So it was appropriate for the town to adopt a stylized mountain and sunburst as their logo. (Author collection.)

After the incorporation of the town, the new town council took up quarters in a newly constructed building on Cochise Road. This building is occupied today by the Rainbow Stained Glass Shop. (Author collection.)

The town offices next moved to a new location on Bob Drive, and a police station was located in the adjoining building. (Author collection.)

In 1999, another move occurred when the town council offices were located in much larger facilities on Civic Circle. Town offices were also opened in this new complex. (Author collection.)

The police station was moved to a much larger facility on Civic Circle next to the civic center. As the town grew, additional space was needed. The complex was named for a former police chief and is now called the Ed Seder Law Enforcement Center. (Town of Prescott Valley.)

prescott valley | yavapai
public library | community college

richärd + bauer, llc

The Prescott Valley Library has operated in many locations. From its beginning in the tiny building that housed the post office, it has moved to the strip mall on Frontage Road, to a building in the Bob Drive complex, and then to the third floor of the civic center. It too has outgrown its space, and a new library is under construction on land west of the town offices. This building will also contain space for Yavapai College. (Town of Prescott Valley.)

The land surrounding the civic center has been the scene of various events, ranging from the World Arts Festival to community gatherings for movies or musical programs to Easter egg hunts, as seen here on a rather cool Easter Saturday. (Town of Prescott Valley.)

Recently the Arts and Culture Committee has begun to exhibit pieces of sculpture around the grounds to promote an appreciation of the arts. Some works of Solon Borglum are also displayed inside the building. (Author collection.)

This recent aerial view of the town shows the growth of Prescott Valley since its beginning in 1966. Shown here is the entertainment district in the foreground, Tim's Toyota Center in the center, the East Campus of Yavapai Regional Medical Center, and the civic center complex. Some of the residential area is seen in the background. (Town of Prescott Valley.)

The entertainment district has become the focal point of the town. Along with Harkins Theater, the entertainment district provides entertainment and restaurants as well as a location for street fairs and musical programs. (Darcy Morger Grovenstein.)

Tim's Toyota Center provides a location for a variety of events. The main event, of course, is the hockey season, in which the Sun Dogs are cheered on by the local crowd. Trade shows, conventions, and graduations are also staged here. (Town of Prescott Valley.)

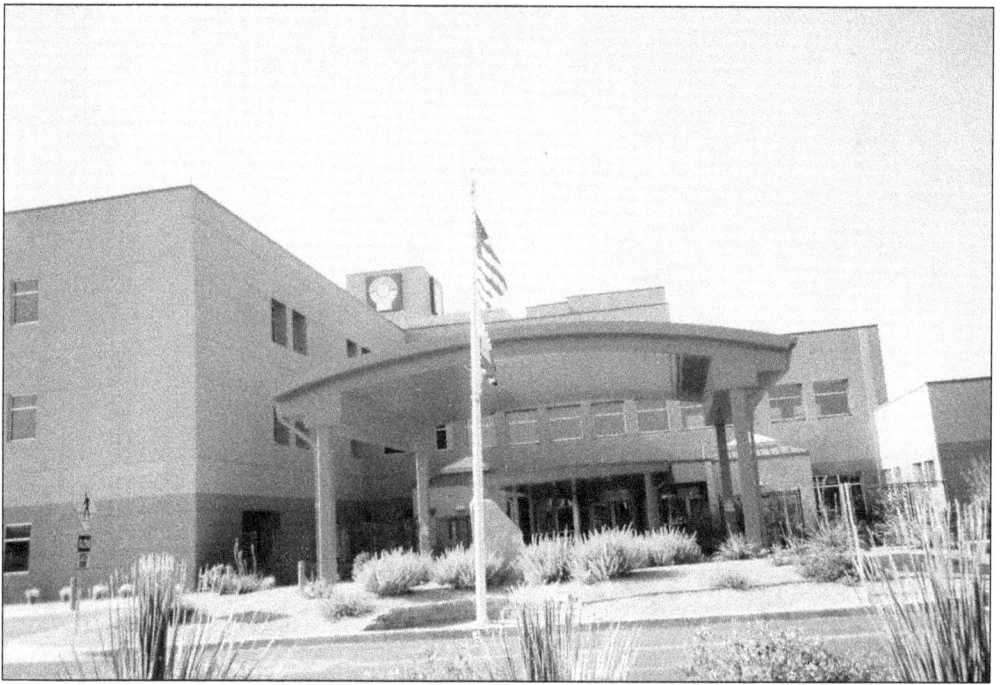

Yavapai Regional Medical Center saw the need for expanded medical facilities. Their East Campus opened in 2005 in Prescott Valley. It is surrounded by various health facilities, including the Del Webb Center. (Town of Prescott Valley.)

Another health facility is located on Windsong Drive. It houses the Mountain Valley Regional Rehabilitation Hospital and offers care for those needing rehabilitation following surgery or injury. (Town of Prescott Valley.)

From the beginning, Prescott Valley has provided for the recreational needs of its citizens. It has 10 public parks. New subdivisions are required to set aside areas for recreation in an effort to promote the well-being of the residents. (Town of Prescott Valley.)

Another medical facility in the area deserves note. The Veterans' Affairs Medical Center is located on Highway 89 north of Prescott. It was formerly Fort Whipple when the Arizona Territory was founded. It has evolved into one of the highest-rated veterans' hospitals in the country. It is no doubt responsible for many of the country's veterans locating in this area. (Author collection.)

The first industry to locate in Prescott Valley was Better Built Aluminum, followed by Print Pack, in the early 1980s. Later an area east of the town was set aside for an industrial park. Ace Hardware Retail Support Center was the first to locate there. This warehouse serves Ace Hardware Stores throughout northern Arizona. (Town of Prescott Valley.)

Industries have found the Prescott Valley area a suitable place to locate. Lockheed Martin has recently located their enterprise in the industrial park near Ace Hardware. It has been joined by several other small businesses. (Town of Prescott Valley.)

Prescott Aerospace is located off Fifth Street near Fain Park. It too recognized that the valley offers advantages not found in other locations. (Author collection.)

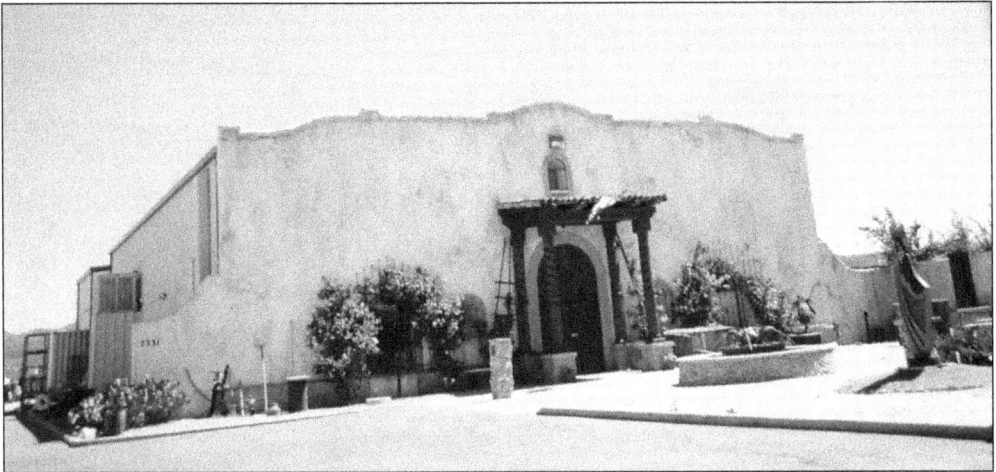

The Bronzesmith Fine Art Foundry, located on Second Street, adds another dimension to the business community of Prescott Valley. Artists of the area and around the country avail themselves of the fine work done here. The foundry offers tours of their establishment to acquaint the public with this unique process. (Author collection.)

Education has always been a concern of area residents. The first school, Lake Valley Elementary School, was built just six years after the founding of the town, and Bradshaw High School followed in 1976 near the Prescott Country Club to serve both Prescott Valley and Humboldt. The town now has over 30 schools, including charter schools, and Bradshaw High School has two campuses. (Author collection.)

An extension of Yavapai College is located along Glassford Hill Road near Bradshaw High School. It will also occupy part of the new Prescott Valley Library. (Author collection.)

From the very beginning of the town, recreation has been a priority. Prescott Valley, Inc., provided a park and swimming pool for the first residents. It also reserved 80 acres in the center of the development for a park. Today the park contains a swimming pool, play areas, soccer fields, a dog park, and an outdoor arena. (Town of Prescott Valley.)

Mountain Valley Park also has two small lakes where once Lake Yavapai was located. These lakes are surrounded by shade trees and a sidewalk for a leisurely walk. Covered picnic tables are also provided. Joggers and dog walkers are often seen making use of this picturesque part of the park. (Author collection.)

Several housing developments have arisen around the town proper. One is located on what has been known as "Jackass Flats" south of town. The Stoneridge development overlooks the town and borders the Bradshaw Mountains. (Town of Prescott Valley.)

Another residential area along Glassford Hill Road has been named for one of the first residents of the valley. Granville Fain, better known as Dan, once ran his cattle here; his descendants are the founders of the Fain Signature Company, which today oversees the commercial growth of downtown Prescott Valley. They also carry on the Fain ranching tradition. (Darcy Morger Grovenstein.)

A banner event in the year 2008 was the acceptance of the Water Deal of the Year Award in London, England, by Larry Tarkowski and John Munderloh. During this year, the town sold 1,003 acre feet of effluent credits to Water Property Investors in a conservation effort. Seen here is Larry Tarkowski (right), Prescott Valley town manager, accepting the award from Nobel Peace Prize winner Muhammad Yunus during the IDA/Global Water Intelligence Conference. (Town of Prescott Valley.)

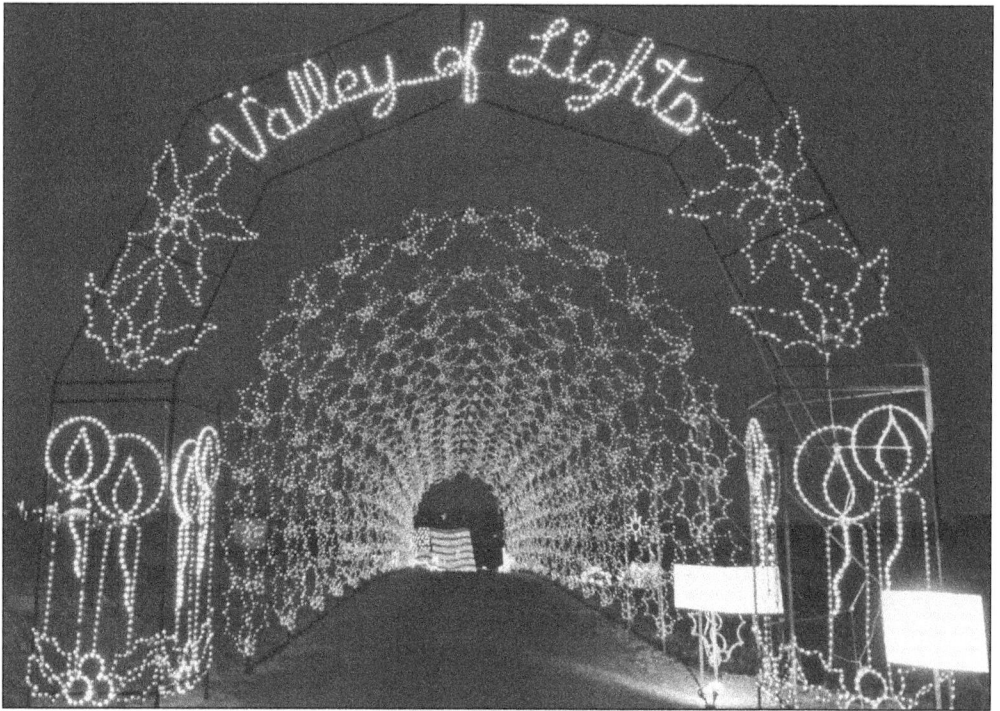

Prescott Valley has become famous for its colorful display of Christmas lights. Animated displays line a road near Fain Park. This lighted tunnel is particularly inviting. (Stew Schrauger/ Natural Visions Photography.)

One of the animated figures depicts an Old West theme as these horses gallop along pulling a stagecoach. (Stew Schrauger/Natural Visions Photography.)

As the population of Yavapai County grew, it became evident the fairgrounds in Prescott could no longer accommodate the county fair. After much discussion, an area in northeastern Prescott Valley along Route 89A was selected as the new location. (Darcy Morger Grovenstein.)

The county fairgrounds are also the scene of horse racing at Yavapai Downs during the summer months. The horses are brought up to cooler climes from Phoenix. (Stew Schrauger/Natural Visions Photography.)

The year 2008 celebrates the 30th anniversary of the incorporation of Prescott Valley. To commemorate the event, this ball was raised on New Year's Eve 2008 amid the explosion of fireworks. Other celebrations are planned throughout the year. (Town of Prescott Valley.)

This sculpture, entitled *Limitless* and created by Michael Tierney, illustrates the growth of Prescott Valley. The artist was impressed with the town's open-mindedness and desire to improve and expand the city. Tierney's Irish family philosophy of living without limits is personified in this sculpture, which seems to reach for the sky and beyond. (Author collection.)

Eight

FAIN PARK

Prescott Valley has provided its citizens with many areas for recreation. The early developers included a park in their plans and provided a swimming pool and picnic area near the A Frame. A section off Robert Road was reserved for recreation and became known as Mountain Valley Park. Small neighborhood parks are scattered throughout the town. New developments are required to reserve an area for a town park. A small park is planned for the Old Town area.

One park highlighted here is a particularly significant area because of its historical background. In 1997, the Fain family donated 100 acres of land along Lynx Creek to the town to be developed as a park. The area is replete with historic landmarks and is more than a recreation area—it is a historic gem.

Within the Fain Park boundaries, one can travel back in history to those people who eked out their living from the environment. Known as the Prescott Culture, these people left the remains of a 27-room pueblo with 24 outlier rooms. It can be visited along one of the trails.

Also within the park is the home of one of the town's first citizens. The Castle, as it is known today, was built in 1890 by Thomas Gibson Barlow Massicks. He was hired by an English company to establish mining operations along the creek. He also founded the town of Massicks near his home.

A chapel was built in 2001 in fulfillment of a dream of Johnie Lee Fain and to preserve the stained-glass windows from the Mercy Hospital once located in Prescott. These windows were in the possession of Henry Brooks, a friend of Johnie Lee Fain. A mining exhibit can also be seen in the park. It contains a restored three-stamp mill and other mining equipment.

Fain Park provides a place to picnic, fish, and hike as well as to become acquainted with Lonesome Valley's history.

One rather unique park in Prescott Valley is located along Lynx Creek, and its land was donated by the Fain family in 1997. Here visitors can spend a peaceful afternoon enjoying the serenity of a very beautiful landscape. (Author collection.)

Birds also find the lake a pleasant place to visit, especially after it has been stocked by the game and fish department. Blue heron are frequent "fishermen," as are ducks and other waterfowl. (Stew Schrauger/Natural Visions Photography.)

An area of the park has been set aside to acquaint the public with the birds found here. Pictures and a list of local birds are on display. This exhibit and other nature exhibits are the work of volunteers Jerry Munderloh and Jean Cross. (Author collection.)

A fishing dock juts out into the lake, and fishermen line its shores. Almost any day, one can see fishermen trying their luck at Fain Park. (Author collection.)

Fain Park is not only for fishing and picnicking, but the hiker also can find trails encircling the lake. Several shorter trails can be found for the visually impaired and physically handicapped. (Author collection.)

A unique feature of the park is its past history. This timeline records the events that have taken place in the area. Prehistoric people once lived along the creek, and later miners took advantage of the rich lodes to be found here. Ranchers ran their cattle in the valley to the north, and farmers planted crops on the fertile banks. The area is being preserved through the generosity of the Fain family and the foresight of the town. (Town of Prescott Valley.)

A 27-room pueblo overlooks the park to the south. Pueblos were rare in the time of the Prescott Culture, as most Native Americans in this region lived in extended family groups in pit houses. It is believed that such large habitations might have been places for ceremonial gatherings. At present, the ruins are not accessible to the public, though tours can be arranged through the parks and recreation department. (Author collection.)

Lynx Creek was dammed up by Barlow Massicks in the 1890s to form a lake for his mining operation. The creek was the scene of many mining claims, and gold panners can often be seen panning for the elusive nugget or just some color. (Author collection.)

This three-stamp mill was part of a mining operation up the creek. In an effort to preserve the history of the mining in the area, Jerry Munderloh and Jean Cross (the author) restored the mill and were responsible for installing it in the park. It was the beginning of the placement of other mining equipment in the park. (Town of Prescott Valley.)

Once the stamp mill was placed in the park, a variety of mining equipment was gathered to extend the exhibit. (Author collection.)

118

This valve was found near the Castle and is believed to have been part of the original dam. The dam can be seen in the background. (Town of Prescott Valley.)

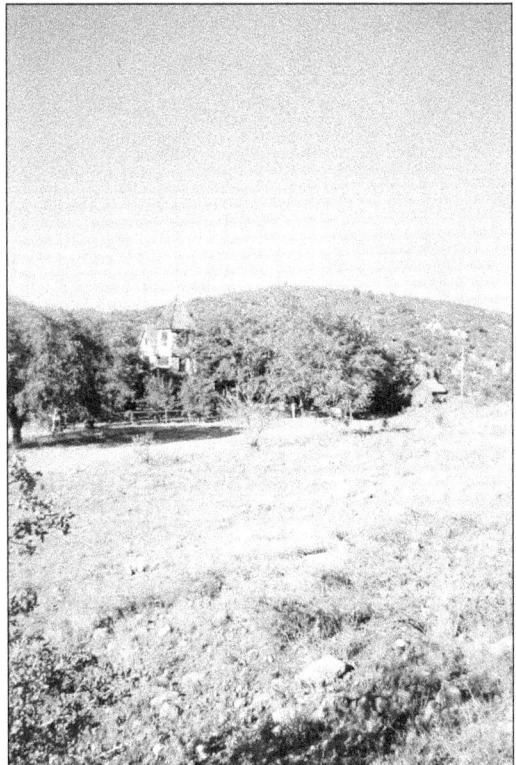

The Barlow Massicks house is also on park property. It was built about 1890 by a young miner employed by a British company to establish a mining operation in the Arizona territory. The house was the scene of many gala events hosted by this rather debonair young man. He often invited the troops from Fort Whipple to enjoy an evening of entertainment. He met an untimely death at the age of 36 after an accidental gunshot wound. (Author collection.)

Another structure within the park boundaries, though on private land, is the Chapel of the Valley. This chapel was dedicated in 2001 and was the dream of Johnie Lee Fain. She had the desire to leave a legacy of lasting beauty for all to enjoy. (Author collection.)

The chapel windows were first placed in the chapel of the Mercy Hospital in Prescott. They were rescued by Henry Brooks when the hospital chapel was to be demolished. Johnie Lee and Henry envisioned the placement of the windows in a chapel along Lynx Creek. The chapel is open to the public on weekends and is often used for private ceremonies. (Author collection.)

Nine

PRESERVATION OF OLD TOWN

In June 2006, after a presentation of the history of Prescott Valley that emphasized the importance of preserving the buildings erected by Prescott Valley, Inc., a group was formed to pursue such a project. It was suggested by author Jean Cross, the presenter of the program, that these buildings could comprise an Old Town District.

This area enjoys great commercial exposure, as it is located on Frontage Road between Robert Road and Navajo Road along Route 69. The Old Town Committee could see the possibility of developing the area as a destination for tourists and local citizens alike. This committee gathered support from the town and the local chamber of commerce. Town officials and knowledgeable people were invited to meetings to familiarize the group with the various aspects involved.

Merchants were contacted to acquaint them with the progress being made and to encourage their participation. The merchants and property owners were skeptical of such a project. In an effort to show its intent, the committee approached the town to establish a park on a small plot of land owned by the town. This became a reality in June 2007. Signs depicting the original use of the buildings have been displayed on all the buildings. The town has placed new street signs on the corners to designate the Old Town area. A street fair was organized in 2007, and merchants were invited to display their wares and open their doors to the visitors.

Realizing the project was becoming a reality, the Old Town Committee reorganized itself and became the Old Town Board. Bylaws were enacted and a 501c3 nonprofit status secured.

Because of all these positive developments, the Old Town is becoming a reality. Further plans for the area are being formulated to make it a destination for all to enjoy.

The buildings erected by Prescott Valley, Inc., in the late 1960s are still occupied by local businesses. They comprise the "historic district" of Prescott Valley. In 2006, a group of citizens saw the need to preserve these buildings and envisioned the area as an Old Town. They have since formed an Old Town Board and have begun work on this worthwhile project. (Author collection.)

The buildings included in Old Town at present are the Prescott Valley Motel, Mingus Motors, the strip mall stores, Oliva's Restaurant, and the Rainbow Stain Glass. (The last is included because of its historic value as the first town hall.) These buildings were built by the company in an effort to show its intent to establish the town and to provide employment for some of the early residents. (Author collection.)

This little building is located in Oliva's parking lot. It once housed the first Prescott Valley Post Office, and before that it was a tack room at the stables. (Author collection.)

A vacant lot between Robert Road and Tani Road has been designated for a town park within the Old Town. It was once the location of Kate King's nursery. Kate was well known for her interest in growing iris plants. She was also the former wife of Norman Romero, one of the early executives of Prescott Valley, Inc. (Author collection.)

The Old Town Board has worked diligently to promote the area as a location for specialty shops. During Prescott Valley Days in 2007, they entered this float in the parade. Three members of the board—from left to right, Patty Lasker, Pat Boone, and Jean Cross—are seen here in front of a replica of one of the shops as it once appeared in the strip mall. (Author collection.)

Because Old Town is located along Frontage Road, it enjoys great exposure to the heavy traffic along Highway 69. Street fairs and other activities are planned in front of the mall. These aim to promote the area and to provide a shopping experience for the public. (Author collection.)

As in the early days when the Valley Plainsmen presented their Old West portrayals during Prescott Valley Days, so the "Shady Ladies" appear here at the first Old Town Street Fair. As Prescott Valley grew from an old-time ranching area, its present-day residents still take delight in such Old West portrayals. The Old Town Board hopes this area will eventually become a historic district and thus preserve the beginnings of the town of Prescott Valley. (Author collection.)

The town has joined in to make Old Town a reality by placing historic signs on each corner to indicate the present boundaries of the district. It is hoped that in the future other areas will become part of the project to preserve and promote the beginnings of Prescott Valley. (Author collection.)

BIBLIOGRAPHY

Hanchett, Leland J. Jr. *Catch the Stage to Phoenix*. Phoenix, AZ: Pine Rim Publishing, 1998.

Maxwell, Margaret. *A Passion for Freedom*. Tucson, AZ: University of Arizona Press, 1982.

Morgan, Learah Cooper, ed. *Echoes of the Past, Volume I*. Prescott, AZ: The Yavapai Cow Belles, 1955.

Potter, Alvina N. *The Many Lives of the Lynx*. Prescott, AZ: self-published, 1964.

Sanders, Thomas. Al Bates, ed. *My Arizona Adventures*. Prescott, AZ: Prescott Corral of Westerners International, 2003.

Sayre, John W. *Ghost Railroads of Central Arizona: A Journey through Yesteryear*. Boulder, CO: Pruett Publishing Company, 1985.

Sheridan, Thomas E. *Arizona—A History*. Tucson, AZ: University of Arizona Press, 1987.

Smith, Dean. *The Fains of Lonesome Valley*. Prescott Valley, AZ: Lonesome Valley Press, 1998.

Stevens, Robert C. *Echoes of the Past, Volume II*. Prescott, AZ: Yavapai Cow Belles, 1964.

Summerhayes, Martha. *Vanished Arizona*. Lincoln, NE: University of Nebraska Press, 1979.

Wuznicki, Robert. *History of Arizona*. Phoenix, AZ: Messenger Graphics, 1987.

www.ingramcontent.com/pod-product-compliance
Lightning Source LLC
Chambersburg PA
CBHW050541110426
42813CB00008B/2224